BABUSHKIN'S CATALOGUE OF
JEWISH INVENTIONS

Text by Lawrence Bush • Illustrations by Richard Codor

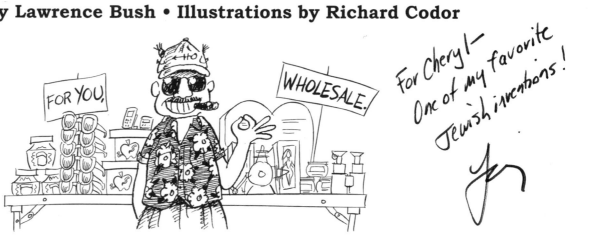

*For Cheryl —
One of my favorite
Jewish inventions!*

Our Guarantee:
At Babushkin's Catalogue, we stand behind our products — way behind!

IF I WERE A RICH CAT
YII-DA ,DAI-DA, DIII...

BABUSHKIN'S CATALOGUE OF
JEWISH INVENTIONS

Lawrence Bush & Richard Codor

with special thanks to Bruce Sager and Susan Griss

Published by Loose Line Productions, Inc.
in cooperation with Blue Thread Communications
P.O. Box 111• Accord, NY 12404
ISBN: 978-0-9799218-2-7
Library of Congress Cataloguing-in-Publication Data is available.
Contact us at babushkinscatalogue@gmail.com

To order: www.haggadahsrus.com, telephone 877.308-4175

"To sell something they want and you've got —
that's not business.

"To sell something they don't want and you haven't got —
now, *that's* business!"

—L.D. Babushkin, founder and president

*All the items in this catalogue are make-believe and not for sale.
Shnook! Didn't you ever hear of mail fraud?*

For Brunyard Yard — L.B.

For Liora's fine tooth comb. —R.C.

Call now! Our operators are waiting to take your money!

Gifts for the Holidays & Special Occasions

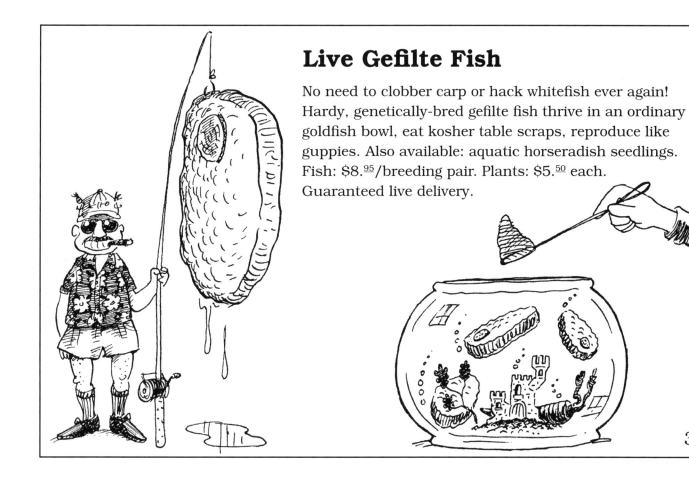

Live Gefilte Fish

No need to clobber carp or hack whitefish ever again! Hardy, genetically-bred gefilte fish thrive in an ordinary goldfish bowl, eat kosher table scraps, reproduce like guppies. Also available: aquatic horseradish seedlings. Fish: $8.^{95}/breeding pair. Plants: $5.^{50} each. Guaranteed live delivery.

3

Climate-Control Khupe

Don't leave it to the heavens to determine the success of your big day! Traditional wedding canopy protects the happy couple from rain, snow, unpleasant weather. Built-in sunlamps work on your honeymoon tan before you've even cut the cake. Precision fans provide air-stream protection on sticky days, avoids embarrassing stains and expensive cleaning bills. Requires assembly. $449.⁹⁵

4

Motorized Hora Hoop

Keeps 'em moving in the same direction!
With wrist straps so nobody loses grip.
Fatigued dancers can dangle, avoid
trampling. Our special musical
hoop plays "Hava Nagila,"
gives the band a break.
Requires assembly.
$139.^{99}

5

Super-Sukkah

Enjoy this most festive festival without the mess and bother of building a sukkah. Super-Sukkah erects your fully-decorated booth as soon as you pull the tab. (Please note: the "holes in the roof" are required by Jewish law.) $369.[95]

How to Spell Ha-noo-ka

In the Second Century BCE, Jews defied their Hellenistic oppressors and created a holiday that defies orthography! At long last, you can learn how to spell the name of the Festival of Lights correctly with this easy-to-read, 613-page book. Paperback, fifth edition. $11.[95]

Sefirotic Tree

You'll never be tempted by a Christmas tree or Hanukkah bush again once you've erected our Kabbalah-style Sefirotic Tree! The whole family can gaze upon Eternity (without going mad!) on those long, dark winter nights. Comes with clear plastic "Yesod" stand and lots of sparkly things. $129.^{95}

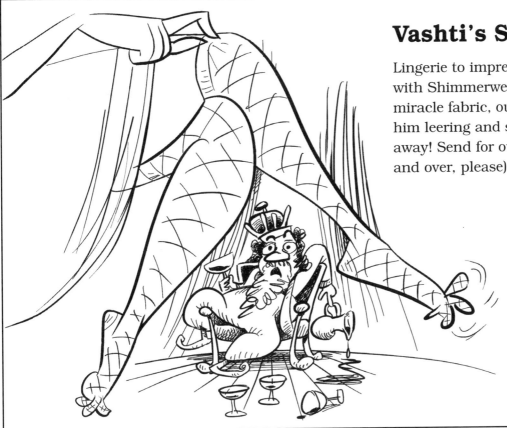

Vashti's Secret

Lingerie to impress a king! Woven with Shimmerwear™, a 21st Century miracle fabric, our fashions will keep him leering and scarem-that-harem away! Send for our catalogue (age 18 and over, please).

Flexodox™ Rabbi

Our life-size Flexodox™ rabbi
bends over backwards to
accommodate your
lifestyle choices.
Firm yet flexible,
impeccably dressed.
$129.^{95}

Extra-Large Grandparents

More of a good thing. Extra-wide lap space.
Arm-span enough to hug the whole family!
$650 each, $1,200/pair.

11

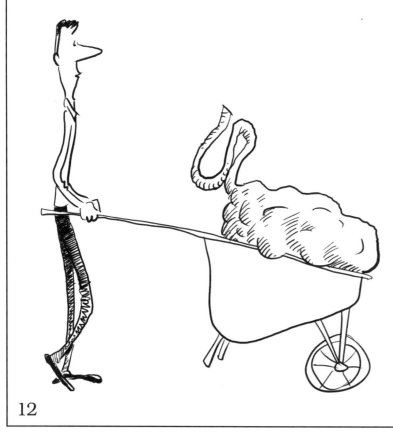

Substitute Stomach ("The Grossinger")

Avoid overeating, even at the most sumptuous affairs. Disposable, lightweight, folds to wallet-size. $19.^{95} Also available, "The Concord," for hearty eaters.*

* Caution: The Substitute Stomach does not digest and is not recommended as a dieting aid.

Prune Soda

"The pause that *really* refreshes."
All natural. $17.⁹⁵/case of 12

13

Fool-Your-Father Inheritance Suits

Never mind lawsuits — disguise yourself with one of our inheritance suits, and ol' Dad (and your rich siblings) will never know what hit 'em! Designed by the Babushkin Costume Studio in Hollywood, MO. Priced as low as $895.*

* Does not include makeup or legal fees. Product is intended for recreational use only. Please check local regulations.

14

Feud Tracker™ App

There's nothing like a family feud to spoil a good funeral. Feud Tracker™ makes sure that folks who never buried the hatchet aren't doomed to an eternity of squabbling. Whether you're a rabbi, social worker, funeral director, or just an innocent daughter-in-law, this app is a must-have guarantor of your peace of mind. $89.^{95}

Furnishings & Gadgets for Home & Office

Personal Boardwalk

A perfect addition to your living room, and a real status item! Complete with knish stand, bench, and water fountain. Weather-worn wood to minimize splintering. Great for bare-footin'! $12,000, requires assembly. Sand optional, $139.^{95}/kilo, one ton minimum.

Burglar Alarm Mezuzah

Sanctifies and protects your home. Hand-crafted brass.
Electronic eye silently detects intruder's presence,
sounds piercing shofar alarm. Regular, $79.^{95}
Deluxe, with smoke detector, $99.^{95}

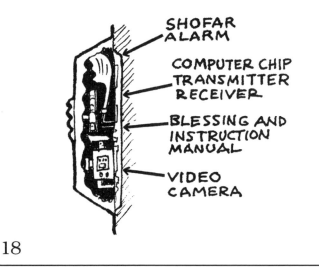

SHOFAR
ALARM

COMPUTER CHIP
TRANSMITTER
RECEIVER

BLESSING AND
INSTRUCTION
MANUAL

VIDEO
CAMERA

Reversible Plates

Trying to keep kosher in a studio apartment? Our reversible plates save cupboard space. Flexible, unbreakable plastic, reverses for meat or dairy meals. Two-toned so you never make a mistake. $88.^{95}/service for six.

1.)

2.) FLEX FLEX

3.) BOING

4.) PLOP

BOING

6.) FLIP

7.) PLOP

19

His and Hers Plastic Slipcovers

Protect yourself and your loved ones from germs, wear and tear. Head-to-toe slipcovers are light, fully transparent, waterproof. Double-reinforced zipper. Available in small, medium and large for children, queen- or king-size for adults. $29.^{95} each, $79.^{95}/family of four.

Electric Davening Board

For the man or woman who has everything.
Variable speed control to suit all, from the
zealot to the mildly observant. Great exercise
aid, too. $49.^{95} (batteries not included).
For Arizona, Florida and Southern California
residents, our solar model, $59.^{95}

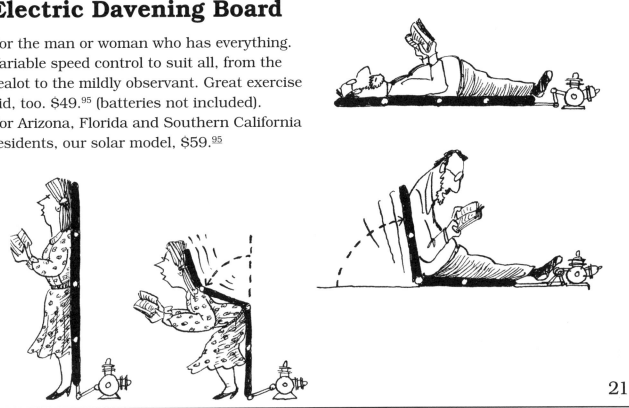

Full House™ Camouflage Kit

There's always a hotel waiting across town when your relatives or unexpected guests see our Full House™ cutouts! Kit includes three different silhouetted "gatherings" that make clear that you've got 24-hour company, and a "Beware of Dog" sign just to make sure! $29.^{95}

The Vault

Madoff made off with billions — and you need old-fashioned protection! The Vault gives you a good night's sleep, every night. Bed-bug resistant. $695; with boxspring, headstand, $995. Extra-large sheet sets for prosperous years: $59.[95]

GUARANTEED 100% MADOFF PROOF

The Rambam Genius Phone™

Why settle for a smart phone when you can have the Rambam Genius Phone™ for only pennies more? Featuring both apps and shmapps, the genius phone gives you global reach and eyes behind your head for ultra-safe and efficient networking, even in your most intimate moments. Used with the Budding Genius™ adapter to plug into your ear, nose, mouth or other orifices for hands-free use. Complete kit (with indentured servitude contract), $399.[95]

Yenta, the Jewish GPS

You think you know better? Fine, go your way and see if we care! Otherwise, Yenta will tell you where to go, and how! So slow down, already . . . and don't drive like your father! $159.⁹⁵

JHarmony™ Software

Find your way to a blissfully happy relationship with a rabbi, before signing the contract. Your synagogue board will be so entranced by JHarmony™ Software, you'll have to drag them off to meetings! Works with any interactive device. $395.^{95}

ⓤ-Vend

Instant Jewish cuisine for the most discriminating palate. Observe the holy days impeccably, wherever you are, with the delicious products of ⓤ-Vend. Prices and portion sizes vary.

Western Wall Message Board

The perfect networking tool for the busy family, and a whole lot more fun than a bulletin board or tabletop. Our miniature Western Wall has cracks for over 100 small slips of paper. $27.^{95}

Lotsa Matzo

Our oversized sheets of matzo have 1001 uses! Comes with Quik-Clean Crumb Vac™. $99.^{95}/20 sheets.

Blood Libel Insurance

Special offer by Mutual of Mt. Zion to our customers. Free descriptive brochure. No company representative will call.

Self-Improvement Aids

Freeze-Dried Nakhes

Add water, get happy. $4.^{95}

Guilt Balm

Rub it in — you'll feel great!
Safe, non-toxic, washes right off.
Roll-on or spray. $8.^{95}

Enlightenment Apples

An apple a day keeps boredom at bay! Delicious, crunchy Garden of Eden apples brings you knowledge of good and evil and much more — while adding 0 points to your WeightWatchers™ score! Fresh-picked, now in season. $19.^{95}/half bushel*

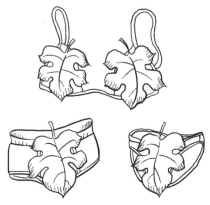

* With your first purchase, get a FREE set of Enlightenment Undies.

34

Judyism

God takes a shave in this feminist retelling of our patriarchal tradition. DVD, $27⁹⁵

35

The WikiWaki Talmud Comic Book!

Learning made simple! Centuries of scholarship in an easy-to-read, colorful comic book, featuring the hijinx of Rabbi Akiva and his rascally gang. Impress your friends. $17.^{95}

Tip-of-the-Tongue Stress Tabs™

Seder or siddur? Kibbitz or kibbutz? Kaddish or kodesh?
Who can keep track of Judaism's weirdly homophonic
language? It's all a matter of where you place the stress.
Tip-of-the-Tongue Stress Tabs™ sharpen your tongue, keep you
from getting stressed out! Just pop two with a glass of seltzer.
$12.^{95}/pack of six

Adopt-a-Doctor

Tired of friends who laud over you the professional accomplishments of their children? Our orphaned M.D.s are eagerly awaiting adoption. Guaranteed to make you puff with pride. Adoption fees (one-time payment): Surgeons, $750; General Practitioners, $450; Podiatrists, $350; Dentists, $125. Soon to be available: Adopt-a-Lawyer.

Cheap Psychoanalysis

Take the cure without breaking the bank.
Eight sessions, $12.^{95} (Sorry, no refunds.)

The Temple Marquee

Your synagogue becomes a Theater Palace when you erect our Temple Marquee out front. Classic, authentic-looking design will have kids pouring into synagogue for their "Saturday Matinee." Lock the doors and they're yours! A realistic kosher candy counter offers tremendous fundraising opportunity for your community. Complete kit, requires assembly, $3,600. (Comes with FREE Flexodox™ Rabbi, see page 10.)

40

Self-Igniting Sabbath Cigarettes

If you must smoke, smoke without sin on the Sabbath!
Crushproof asbestos box. Carton, $24.^{95}

41

The Sweatshop

After feasting on those rich Jewish foods, sweat it out, without leaving home! Babushkin's Sweatshop will set up shop in your spare room and lock you in! Machinery galore, aggressive "trainers," a quota to fill — you'll be a regular Samson! Complete, $1,200

The Nobell Prize

If Henry Kissinger deserved one, so do you! Everyone knows about Jews winning those coveted Stockholm prizes, but not everyone knows how to spell. Fool your friends and impress your tenure committee with our "Nobell" Prizes (with authentic documentation and videotaped ceremony). Sorry, no cash awards. Complete kit, $239.^{95}

For Kids, 8-80

Gag Kasha Varnishkas

The kasha is real, but the bowties are rubber! Harmless latex. Fool your friends. $3.^{95}/12-oz. box, "serves" six.

Baby Siddur

Goo-goo . . . gaaa . . , Sh'ma!
Our Baby Siddur minds your
little ones — and grows their
minds! — with stimulating Jewish
activities. Soothes gums, too, with
safe, non-toxic materials. $44.[95]

Little People of the Book

Babushkin's Goldene Book series. $8.^{95}/each; catalogue available on request.

You *Ate Up* Our Classic Stuffed Cabbage Kids

Adopt these one-of-a-kind dolls as they escape from the Soviet Union. Lovable, washable, $35.^{95} **SORRY, OUT OF STOCK**

Now Meet
Intermarriage Barbie

The world's most popular shikse comes ready to raise the kids Jewish! Kit includes Intro to Judaism Curriculum, discarded Christmas tree, and that Hanukkah Ham you've all been trying to forget! Lots more gear available. $29.^{95}

Old Country Shtetl Kit

Explore your roots with our (Lego™-compatible) Old Country Shtetl Kit. 1,000 pieces, includes shacks, pushcarts, rabbis, matchmakers, schnorrers, potatoes, scrawny calf, mounted Cossacks. $22.^{95}

"Saith the Lord" Prophecy Box

Hanging out on street corners is a whole 'nother thing with our "Saith the Lord" Prophecy Box. Complete with smoking oven, flaming torch, fiery chariot, fire extinguisher, and dire warnings from all parts of the globe. $18.^{95}

Solomon's Judgment Fair-Share™ Knife

Teach those quarrelling kids how to share with our Fair-Share ™ Knife. Comes in a hard, securely locked Temple Sanctum Case™ to prevent accidents and crimes of passion. $149.^{95}

Wide-Awake Father

Alert, involved, supportive — he pays attention!
Guaranteed not to fall asleep in the presence of
company. Generous with loans and gifts.
Regular, $599.[95] Deluxe, with extra set of
car keys, $699.[95]

Dial-a-Mom

We'll call her for you,
report on your progress,
Sundays, holidays.
$900./month,
minimum six months
of service.

Pinch Deflectors

For cheeks and tushies. Spares you the pain and embarrasment that often accompanies family celebrations. Lipstick-resistant, too. Choose from our designer looks: rouged or natural, dimpled or smooth. Kit includes tenderizer, applicator, cleanser. Complete, $14.^{95}

54

Yiddishkite

Fly your Jewish identity before the world! Star of David kite with alef-beyt tail. Sturdy mylar construction. Requires assembly. $17.$^{95}

Finicky Cat?

Try Our

Chai Lives Katz Food

Jewish cuisine for cats. Flavors: Lox 'n' Eggs, Chopped Liver, Sabbath Meal, Herring Platter, Salami 'n' Eggs, Chicken Soup. $25.^{95}/case of 24.

Herring Incense

Available in two enticing scents, shmaltz or matjes.
Long-burning. $5/package of 18 sticks.

Tools for the Adventurous

Transliteration Specs

Turns Hebrew or Yiddish characters into English letters, instantly! Perfect gift for travellers to Israel or for the nervous bar or bat mitzvah. Regular, $12.[95] Tinted, with sports strap, $18.[95]

WhozaJew Stamp Kit

Concerned about being accepted as a Jew? Worried about the immigration desk at Ben-Gurion Airport? Babushkin's WhozaJew Stamp Kit, with our patented Riyadh Rejecter Stamp™, will convince all authorities — even your haredi in-laws! — that you belong to the tribe! $39.[95]

Jihad Ejection Suit

Don't let a suicide bomber ruin your day! Our ejection suit takes you out of the blast range, pronto! The secret is in the Samson-Spring™ Shoes. Suit has built-in parachute. Dry clean only. $119.$^{95}

Kneejerk Support Hose

Blue and white, one size fits all. $11.^{95}/pair.

Palestinian Solution

Our own secret formula. $9.^{95}

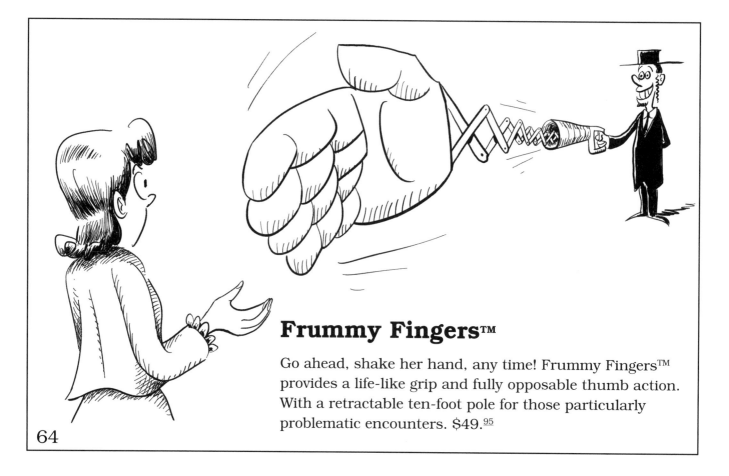

Frummy Fingers™

Go ahead, shake her hand, any time! Frummy Fingers™
provides a life-like grip and fully opposable thumb action.
With a retractable ten-foot pole for those particularly
problematic encounters. $49.[95]

Matchmaker Noodles

The meal that ends with a kiss . . . and a promise of Jewish continuity! Our six-foot egg noodles are delicious, resilient and glatt kosher. Six-foot box (10 noodles) is covered with homey recipes and dating tips, stores easily in closet or golf bag. $10.[95]

Bathsheba Spy Specs

Even in the smoggiest town, our laser-guided spy specs detect rooftop activities and zero in, from up to a mile away! Comes with fancy note cards for special invitations. (Sorry, our Spy Specs are not available to customers under 18 or to registered sex offenders — and don't think we don't know.) $79.^{95}

Vildeh Chaya Wilderness Adventures

Idolatry, anyone? Forty days and forty nights; we provide everything but the sandals and the psychotherapy. $3,600 per individual; family rates available but not recommended.

67

Power-Pocket Pita

This baby carries the entire meal, with condiments and utensils, and travels as comfortably as a fanny pack. Delicious, nutritious, and enormous! $18.^{95}/bag of six.

Loving Chaim Yankl

Don't let Leviticus ruin your happiness:
Stonewall, not stoning, is the new you!
Babushkin's MAN-ual of gay marriage is
both informative and hot! $24.⁹⁵

Kabalalalala

You want intimacy with God? Here goes! The ten classic sefirot (manifestations of the Divine) multiply to hundreds or even thousands in Babushkin's Kabalalalala System of Mystical Union™. Tune in and turn on with ancient-style amulets, ankle bracelets, and trance music. Guaranteed to bring you unbearably close to the Presence or your money back! $119.[95]

Learn to be Human at Mentsh U!

Our six-session certificate course equips nudniks, shlemils, shlemazls, shmuks, shtarkers, ganefs, and other no-goodniks to bring pride to the Jewish community. Mentsh U instructors have been trained on Wall Street and accepted their community-service sentences graciously. Sliding scale fees depend on degree of student's incapacity; free evaluation.

71

Guide for the Clueless: a Glossary

Bathsheba: a woman from one of the "good parts" of the Bible.

blood libel: traditional anti-Semitic slander that Jews need the blood of a Christian child to make matzo — as if our own children's blood were not good enough!

davening: praying while getting jiggy with it.

frummy: ultra-observant, i.e., obsessive-compulsive.

gefilte fish: a blend of carp, whitefish and glop.

haredi: make-believe Amish people.

hora: step, cross in front, step, cross in back — that's an awful lot of crosses for a Jewish dance.

kabbalah: the mystical system of extracting money from Madonna.

kasha varnishkas: buckwheat groats and bowties, slathered with varnish.

khupe (sounds like "hookah"): traditional wedding canopy (sounds like "canapé").

kosher: traditional Jewish dietary law forbids mixing meat and dairy in the same meal because a cheeseburger made Rabbi Judah HaNasi nauseous in 196 CE.

mentsh: what you wish you'd met at Match.com.

mezuzah: an ornament that marks Jewish homes for mob violence.

nakhes: the emotion that prevents your parents from giving you up for adoption.

sefirot: aspects of the Godhead as described in the Zohar and other traditionally insane texts.

shtetl: where Cossacks go to celebrate.

shikse: a woman named Mary or Cristina.

siddur: a book with too much Hebrew in it.

Solomon: Biblical king who determined the identity of a baby's mother by proposing to cut the baby in half. The mother begged him not to, while the other woman asked him to prepare several steaks and please remove the bones.

sukkah: the booth traditionally used for the observance of sukkot.

sukkot: the word traditionally confused with sukkah.

Talmud: centuries of rabbinic discussion, written in Aramaic for easy access.

tzitzit: traditional fringed garment inspired by Davy Crockett.

Vashti: Ancient feminazi: Asked by the king to dance stark naked in front of his friends, she refused!

Vildeh Chaya: a wild woman in our chaste, secure and highly civilized world.

Coming in Our Next Catalogue

Uncle Misha's Ant Kibbutz
Making the deserts bloom with worker ants and HaMalka, the mighty Queen.

Shikse Mixer
Great brew for a Wandering Jew. Please drink responsibly, only not tonight!

Tax Shelter Mezuzah
Sanctifies and protects your moolah, wherever you stash it!

Vegan Chicken
The chicken eats a vegan diet — and you eat the chicken. Deeelish!

L.D. Babushkin, winner of the 2010 Nobell Prize in Creative Economics (see p. 43), has been enlivening Jewish life since the days of yore, and even pre-yore, with gotta-have-it inventions inspired by the Torah and Talmud, pharmaceuticals and comfort food. He has traveled the world from Brooklyn to Queens and places in-between in search of the purest ingredients, finest quality manufacture, and recently lapsed patents in order to present you with the most innovative aids to the modern Jewish lifestyle.

Lawrence Bush is the editor of *Jewish Currents* magazine and the author of *Bessie: A Novel of Love and Revolution; American Torah Toons: 54 Illustrated Commentaries;* and *Waiting for God: The Spiritual Explorations of a Reluctant Atheist,* among other books. His essays and fiction have appeared in the *New York Times, Tikkun,* the *Village Voice,* and *MAD.* Bush writes a short daily blog about the date in progressive Jewish history (*http://jewishcurrents.org*). The first year's entries have been compiled into a new book, JEWDAYO.

Richard Codor makes a living drawing humorously. He is the co-creator and illustrator of the cartoon *Joyous Haggadah, All You Want to Know about Sabbath Services: A Guide for the Perplexed,* and the children's book, *Too Many Latkes!* Codor does storyboards for children's animated movies, TV shows and advertising. He is a recipient of the Jewish Press Association/ Rockower Award for Cartooning and the Charles Schulz Prize. He makes his home in Brooklyn. You can see his work at *www. joyoushaggadah.com* and *http://littleblogofjewishhumor.com/*